Then Yeses Come Bubbling

I0531308

Poems

Ryan Van Lenning

ISBN: 979-8-9934900-8-3

WildNatureHeart.com

Other Books By the Author

for the unbridled Yes

CONTENTS

ASKING THE IMPOSSIBLE

"In nature, creativity is just existence, flowers bloom, and feathers shed. Life breathes and every bird sings. Stones glisten and light change color. Existence is art."
—Xenia Vira

Yeses That You Own

Go through all the othered Yeses
To uncover thundered No's

They are but the bottom side, no less
Than the Yeses that you own.

(Repeat until thick and moist and your voice comes
out clean)

Ruthless As Any Angel

Ruthless as any angel
you asked for a commitment
in your radical way.

It was all or nothing—
so with a deep roar
I said Yes.

Yes! I said it.

Then Yeses came bubbling
off my skin like water boiling
flying off like mist

Yeses arrived like dancing worms in dirt
breaking down the old and scented world

I understood the terms of the agreement
marked with that ecological Yes,
echoing effervescent:

All that is not aligned must fall away
You shall abandon all the false homes

I may wake you at all hours, like a lover;
With but a touch, you'll respond

my whisper will be your watchword
and you shall empty yourself for me

all the terrifying and beautiful beasts
will be your friends

3

we shall make a flowing river of glaciers
and dust off the moon

the overwhelming fountain of things
will pour into and out of us

things as pure as a spider bite
a horse kick

a pomegranate dawn
a lightning strike

a broken bone
a new kiss

will sing themselves into the stardust world
as medicine and muse.

Yes!

Signed with black feather in rainbow ink,
-me

What Can We Expect From a Poem?

An elucidation
making hidden things manifest

a jolt, a revolution
a delicious meal
a top-40 hit

a burgundy sea-shell among the grey
a meteor shower
walking you home with an arm around your waist
make you feel something,

anything.

To invite you to face something you'd rather not face
too much - tell the poem to get lost

a laugh or tear
a grunt or grimace
a sadness, a joy
some thin strand of hope

to see something new
as through a soft portal

to see something old from the underbelly
to see something from inside of the mitochondria
from the point of view of a worm
from the uvula-a-a-a-a hanging

a reason to revolt, to live
like waves crashing relentlessly against the shore
no end in sight

to chart the globe
a wordy longitude
blessed rage for order

to be a culture maker, a world maker
making it make me make you

but what if it just asks a question
with no answer given?

what then?

Photosynthetic Crescendos of Longing

I ask the impossible: that every line
be as anchored as acrobatic

as dense with gravity as it is buoyant
with light, rippled through

with a graceful severity
like that moment of leporine surrender

to the falcon's talons
after a lifetime of darting away

as robust as an egg, heating up
not just the shell, but the yolk of it

when cracked open you find yourself
richly hitched to every note

stumbling into the not-so-secret
sacred symphony of things

where both the dark descending arpeggios
and photosynthetic crescendos of longing

make the music
and the music is all there is, revealing

that the turn towards the tender
is a tune tied to the pull of the promise

of utter devastation and wholeness
without a final resolution, but revealing

that the center of the earth
and whatever makes the surface

of the sun dance
are equally home—

An impossible request I know, yet
here we are, breathing, living it

and if we're not here for impossible things...

Gorgeous Storm

This gorgeous storm
keeps getting stuck in my teeth

as if I could bite-size my way
to destiny

when all I want
is to have it come
racing out my lungs

like a waterfall plunging
over my luscious tongue

flooding all the landscapes
of my crooked life.

When all I want is to join the wrens and warblers
and beloved lusts of a wounded world
washing away the old debris

Please, Storm, please,
knock down the weak branches
of my being

Prune me for the season
I am meant to live

To Begin

To begin
requires a leaping

not a crawling,
a creeping,
nor a sleepwalking

It is said:
you get to the top of the mountain
step by precious step

It's true – I've proved the theory.

But to find YOUR mountain
to decide to walk it
with the authority of your two feet

that is the Leap

and then to commit
to not returning
to the old place

So stand up and put on your jumping shoes

whether it's a soft or hard springing board
is irrelevant

If your heart is ready: Leap!

Leap up and lick the sky
with the genius of your inimitable heart.

10

Burn Your Yeses and Accept the Consequences

"Give me silence, water, hope. Give me struggle, iron, volcanoes." —Pablo Neruda

Some questions can only be asked from glass mountains. Built from boulders of obsidian.

Building huts on the side of volcanoes is risky business. Pumice cuts into bare feet; wind sculpts your soul.

Sky promises everything and gravity teaches humility. These become lessons worth the beastly bruises.

Aren't we lucky to have as allies not only erosion and digestion, not only insemination and pollination, but Eruption?

Eruption means nothing less than the end of the world as we know it. It is a feral force honoring the wisdom that old containers must die.

Eruption is an ultimate gesture of faith in the Unknown.

Eruption screams 'I'm not afraid to lose everything for something new and real!"

Yet any path requires consequence. Sometimes consequence is a kiss, sometimes collapse.

Or upheaval, a cindered landscape, or Uncertain Skies.

A question flowing down the caldera:

11

Are we willing for our heart-eggs to be cracked open by consequences?

We don't have to say Yes.

But we must say Yes to the consequences of either saying No or saying Yes.

What about Maybe?

It's true, we can dither with weak-kneed maybes. Yet Maybes are ways of dancing on the rim of the caldera anyway.

We can dither 'til we die—Either way we'll be right. Either by eruption or a collapsing or erosion, we'll be right.

This thing called Comfort - you hear a lot about it during eras of forgetfulness and paved over rivers.

What is not allowed to be heard: Comfort is a killer. The murderer they never caught.

No one asks: What if everything is already lost when we gain everything we thought we wanted?

Again, some questions can only be asked from glass mountains.

If you look closely, you'll find lichen even on lava and understand—
the real conspiracy is towards Life.

If you're one of those who pretends a saccharine peace, imagining Life doesn't require violent explosion, consider the Sun.

What is a volcano other than Sun in the earth?

What is lichen other than a way to worship a star?

And what is a menacing question other than a fireball in your heart?

We fall to our knees:

We, crooked creatures, err on the side of dirt and fire.

We, alive ones, burn with our Yeses
and accept the consequences.

We, beautiful beasts, open to the opening Earth.

Mystery of Emergence

All of sudden it appears:

The blossom. The catkin. The dawn.

The clarity. The intuition. The bubbling up
of daylighted grief.

The surprise courage. The gratuitous laughter. An
unexpected crush.

The crack. The vision beyond. The rooted purpose.

The surprising hatchlings in the nest of your heart.

What was absent or hidden from plain sight, now with
the right conditions announces itself as if it were always
there, a bold and necessary part of the whole world.
And it is necessary.

This is the Mystery of Emergence.

Of course, we suspect it never really disappeared, but
had merely gone underground a while, nurtured by the
fruitful darkness, by the necessary and fertile rest. It had
perhaps been extending its hidden rhizomes through
the body of the earth, through your body, awaiting the
appropriate time.

We may find that some Emergences are so utterly new,
so unlike what came before, they catch us by
surprise—So we must be there, like a birth doula, to
catch them.

This is the Mystery of Emergence.

So here we are. We slowly emerge (or leap!) from our winter dens and old forms. It had its harshness; it had its creature comforts. But Life and light beckon.

Liberation calls, and we become hungry for expansion, for play, for worlds beyond the old. For planting love where the dragons of fear lay.

Our dreams have been incubating—They, too, will not bare being covered forever.

Our role is to tend. To continue to cultivate them with intention. With the proper tending, these micro-blossomings may grow into their fullness, feeding the world and the Grand Metabolism with beauty, calories, heat, and perhaps a little sweetness.

This is the Mystery of Emergence.

What seeds of deep imagination or embodied truth are sprouting in you, asking for tending?

Which ones help lead us all beyond Empire?

Or as adrienne maree brown expresses it in the context of deep time: "How can we, future ancestors, align ourselves with the most, resilient practices of emergence as a species? We embody. We learn. We release the idea of failure because it's all data. But first we imagine. What are the ideas that will liberate all of us?"

This is the Mystery of Emergence.

Rave On Bold Scratchers

Stretch big and rave on bold scratchers.

Stretch out towards the world pouring in
trying to capture the endless bouquets
of beauty and pain

Scratch black and white shapes
and florid brushstrokes on our canvasses
conjure melodies like mad magicians

all the while knowing they're mere clouds
blowing through
like transient guests on vacation.

Like everything.

One day we'll sit with the final sunset
with only the merest scratch
in the sand remaining

and even that will be
reclaimed by the great sea at midnight—
just as we will be.

Yet still we stretch and scratch.

We are alive.

Stretch big and rave on bold scratchers.

Catching Gnats With a Butterfly Net

Everything is a metaphor for everything else
and language the jewel in our crown.

Yet words are too flimsy a net
to catch their subject—
like trying to catch gnats with a butterfly net.

These ancient gossamer handkerchiefs,
spun from fine thread of speech,
tossed casually or in earnest
over barbed wire
falls apart at the slightest touch.

Compared to a purple artichoke flower
or the tentacles of an octopus
a perfect golden ear of corn
the canopy of the giant sequoia
a Midwest thunderstorm
words are such a silly, subtle way
to express or "capture" anything.

Even the lowly paramecium
is more real than these words.

But that's what we do—our gift,
so profligate with words
like semen and salmon eggs
endlessly ejaculating.

The vast majority never find their target,
don't fertilize, never develop.

Dead on arrival.

17

Even the most poignant poem
or soaring Shakespearean sonnet
is the muddy bottom
of a mountain meadow
through which the real river flows over
forever beyond our grasp
like sand through fingertips.

Wait! But all that's a big lie
spun from a truth.

I've caught myself
in my own spider web. Just a cover
like the spots of a leopard,
the shell of a hermit crab.

Rather: even the lowliest adjective
the most sluggish worm of a word,
the most simple sentence,
awkward and misplaced
is no different than the horse's gorgeous mane
or the horsehead nebula.

The kitschiest contrived love letter
the most melodramatic sarcastic slam poem
is no less a marvel
than the courtship ritual of penguins
the melody of a mourning dove
the mating of jungle frogs.

So flimsy nets words may be
but like sunflowers and sweet peas
striving towards the Sun
they reach ever upwards and outwards...

Of Spore and Storm

Bereft of the energy of withholding
abundance will take care of itself

like those countless spores
on the belly side of fern friends
or mushrooms the shape of private parts
commuting on the wind.

But they're not private.

They're out there for the whole world
in teeming pomp and pageant

like the passing storm
handing out droplets
to every eager passerby
not holding back anything.

So Yes, be the wild and wetness.
Becoming wild and wet, be the Yes.

Be the spore and storm
in boundless beneficence—

There's no chance of failing then.

Things Were Built

Before I arrived, flint ax and fire
fences and fine fishing wire

Long canals and solid streets
Mathematical proofs, monumental feats

Towers upon cathedrals upon burial mounds
giant gears with steely sounds

(more dead empires than can be found)

But my sacred soars even more
with avian bells and dawn's decor

With wild Mustard, a monument
And Teasel a temple with purple tint

and Egret, gentling paintbrush wings
over cattails and quiet things,

I remember as she gifts her flight, that
nothing I build can be so right.

Recite the Eons Long Poem In Your Blood

"I believed I wanted to be a poet,
but deep down I just wanted to be a poem."
~Jaime Gil de Biedma

There comes a moment when you stand stunned at the edge of the Unfurling and suddenly grok:

with what delicious devotion deep time has been carving the canyons of you with its undying rivers of consequence coursing through them, pouring that eons-long poem through your blood and you are confronted with your favorite fear—to die without having recited it.

And if you know anything at all it is this: you must embrace that relentless allegation of your miraculous destiny with each unearned breathe.

That you are no dead dust mote settled, that you must under-take the ritual of foraging from the brambles of time the forbidden meter of your love, your elemental kick, soaring and sibylline, stirred up like a once-in-a-life-time comet, flashing in dark skies.

Gig Is Up

The gig is up, put on your whale ears.

There are words in this desert
older than your grandmother

older than the grandmother tree
in your grandmother's dreams.

"Loudly for Truth have liars pled,
their heels for Freedom slaves will click"

Bend low your cheek to fox's den
to hear a flock of clicks and then
a cute collapse, eat all the sins

If you find us, you will find us
in the Strange Curiosities Tent
at the Festival of Slow Surrendering

"where Boobs are holy, poets mad,
illustrious punks of Progress shriek"

We'll be playing a game of letting go
with all the Heretic Hilariums

"when Souls are outlawed, Hearts are sick"

And skipping rocks at the bulbs
in the billion-watt culture

'Cause when peace requires a mass grave
and a thousand prisons
one's core job is to disturb the peace.

"If Hate's a game and Love's a fuck"

The first rule of Compost Club
is to lend back your tears.

"Hearts being sick, Minds nothing can"

The second rule of Compost Club
is to cook it with the heat
of your awe-full truth-telling.

You can tell it with your face,
or with your dumb gut
but we ain't going nowhere
without a bit-a-cookin'

We'll be in the Castle with No Walls
poking fun at the king's long nose

"who dares to call himself a man?"

Giving out the same advice
we give our inner tyrant:

Abdicate the throne, sell the Crown Jewels for dust
on your shins

Don't skip the big party,
you tasty freak.

Caress the edges, hold the sharp
and soft orbits.

Be a big flea, make us jump.
Scratch your deepest itch.
Throw us your exuberant pollination,

lend us your scent.

Let us hear your ultrasonic rat giggles—
keep us up at night,
dancing and dabbling
in the spark arts.

We need them—the Show must go on.

*italicized quotes from E.E. Cummings' 'Jehovah
buried, Satan dead'

IMAGINATION IS BEYOND DESPAIR

"If you find your imagination cannot stop itself from churning out the scripts of the Death Machines, pull its plug. Dismantle it. Reprogram it. Dream Daylight. Manufacture Daylight. We are the Magicians. Make Magic." —Krista Franklin, "Call"

The Artisan

I. WELCOME

The artisan is working on me
in her open atelier.

Welcome, she says,
This is the city of floating fog
quarried from the nearest
and the far.

One cannot see across
to the other side,
but the world here is quite enough,
enough for the wild ride.

She's carving and cooking me
with hands skilled
and hanging like a hemlock's art.

Fashioning grooves to drain my fumbled head
creating a humble watershed instead

assembling little bold me,
rich with rain.

II. BREAKING DOWN

It's time to have a conversation with mud.

Do not resist the season of broken earth,
inside an era of air.

There is no alone.

We've been shown:
even a mountain is a cloud
and mud must be
a species of all of us.

Be patient with your breaking down.

III. A QUERY

Q: Am I decomposing or re-composing now?

Can I close my hands around it all somehow?

A: No, there's no holding it—
There's only weaving through the spaces.

And it's all spaces.

Don't worry about grasping,
we're misting together in our core.

You'll open your fists and find it all there.

IV. LESS ANVIL THAN ANNUAL SOIL

She's working on me—
breaking me down with fungi sighs
her out-breath of a million skies.

Last night she dropped a river
right to my bottom, a temporary nest.

Ok, I'll hover here for a moment—
an eon perhaps—for even clouds repose
and have to eat, I suppose.

V. TRANSPOSE TO WE

At times we eat by taking in
and other times by entering
and now we want inside of you.

For you, we are a meal.

Open up—say ahhhh!!!

Ahhhh....We're assembling an artisan
in our open air lair.

Our calories will form
some small part of that slick poem in you.

And we mustn't forget the vowels,
like clouds connecting the consonants
of your crooked mountain peaks.

VI. ALL THAT'S GREEN AND PURE
POURS THROUGH

At dawn I'm new again
like you.

We're assembling an artifact—
We want you and you and you.

No Less a Web, Spider Spun

No less a web, spider spun
these words around you weaving run
like threads so fine, but not less strong
to bind within you magic songs

And here a peek behind the art
a secret with which no spider parts
Yet I, a weaver of open source
share a bit of that conjuring force

See clear, my witches, an image bold
with which your sticky tales told
float it in your inner sea
and with all your eyes, like spiders see

Make of yourself a giant ear
and gather all the things you hear
and let love be greater than deepest fear
and you'll find that threads appear

> Ask what it is you want to net
> with ever spinning spidery set
> you just might catch it yet

Full flinging into nothingness
is what it takes—nothing less
With feral trust and no reason why
your filament will find its flight

Once it's flung, that's but half the spell
the other half is crafting well
circle 'round and join the threads
and paint the image in your head

In between, a tip or three:
a spell, to weave, is both form and free

Threads are summoned from abdomen
but also from the wild winds
a gentle breeze will be your friend
a gusty gale will be your end

> *unless you surf that storm with ease*
> *you'll wind up in the web you weave*

See what other orbs construct
see what's cast, and see what's luck
Admire patterns, see what's caught
Look for angels and demons fought

> *Look to the recluse, the widow, the wood,*
> *but never get caught in the net of 'should'*

Take what you can, as in a sly theft
but the strength of your web is bound by what's left
after all of the threads from within are out-cast
into the world to feast or to fast

That something so strange, something so rich
that deep design only you can pitch
that something so rich, so doubly strange
things may be caught quite out of your range

> *A final glimpse behind the weave*
> *before we rest and take our leave*

As silence is part a wizard's gift
what's not said will shape and shift
the space between the strands are there
to make designs in air appear

> *more luminous and boldly spun*
> *as much for purpose as for fun*

And as spiders in their patience sit
awaiting what their net can get
so our last secret of this webby play
will have to wait another day.

The Undressed Yes

For the No, I'll stay restrained
Remaining all the same old strange
But for the Yes that feels fleshed
I'll be the New that's awed-ly blessed

For the Yeses that are weak
I'll be the claw, I'll be the beak
Pecking at the no's and nots
Tearing all those noisy knots

For the Yes that is still stuck
I'll take my talons, rip it up

But for the unbridled Yes
I'll chirp like the first-born bird
Singing up the morning light
Until the sun itself takes flight

For the Undressed Yes indeed
I'll beat every wing in me
With all my rainbow feathers flocked
Turning all my rocks to hawks

And for the best and brightest Yes
I'll bring the most creative caress

I'll be the falcon fearless flying
I'll be the cosmic Heart undying

I'll be the eagle eye so keen
To Soar the Greatest Show yet seen.

Instructions For Making a Perfect Ker-Plunk

The first thing you're gonna wanna do
is find yourself the prefect river-fed pool.

If you're looking for a rainbow,
the colored stones on the bottom
will do just fine

Spiced with white and black stones
on the edge
where you will sit and stick your feet in.

You'll notice the volcanic gneiss
the river falls over
looks a like a miniature mountain range.

You'll also be forgiven for mistaking them as waves.

I assure they are not waves
—at least not of water—
as tested against my shin and skin.

But perhaps they are just very slow moving waves
harder than water, softer than diamond.

The liquid portion of the river sneaks
around and over and through these.

The technique I will show you
will have you making perfect ker-plunks
within three hours. Four tops.

Be sure to have eaten beforehand.

Find a medium-sized rock, preferably round.

Too large and it'll sink quickly
giving you a little blump,
without the ka-
which is really the whole point.

Too small and you'll get a quick
high-pitched blump or plunk.

Find one the size of a child's heart.
If it's beating, even better.

Now, you'll want to find the perfect depth.
Too shallow or too deep
and you'll find yourself in the wrong register.

You're going for medium to low range,
with a healthy splash.

If a blue dragonfly comes by
asking what you're doing,
just smile and say, "Experimenting."

They'll know.

After all, they are the ones who invented
tandem aerial fornication—
so yeah, they get experimentation.

The water bugs seem used to this sort of thing.
They'll scatter for a few seconds, then re-congregate,
riding the ripples.

By this time, you'll notice the changing light,
and subsequent patterns on the water,

creating stretch marks up the taller trees
and flip-flops of green and black
on the smaller ones.

While trunks of firs become giant worms
grey and gyrating.

Don't be alarmed. They rarely bite.

Once you get a dozen or so ka-blumps in a row,
you'll notice a peculiar, but healthy side effect:

Concentric circles emanating
from where your child's heart ker-plunked

ring upon ring
gently lapping at your ankles
ring upon ring
leaping up your torso
ring upon ring
inside you.

Can you feel them?

Take Up Your Wand

*"If one [the conductor] uses a baton, the baton itself
must be a living thing, charged with a kind of
electricity, which makes it an instrument of meaning in
its tiniest movement." —Leonard Bernstein*

It matters not the noise of the crowd.

How might that mindless cacophony
even approach your perfect pitch?

Let the noise be a Nothingness to you.

Chop off your ears, if you must, Maestro
and hear the charm of the music
born of bones within.

Take up your wand in hands majestic molded
and conduct your own sacred symphony.

Stir the oboes from their solemn slumber
put to sleep by the loud trumpeters,
roguish assassins of the soul.

Pick up your baton, Blessed Conductor—
let your left hand be the rhythm of the dusk and dawn
and your right hand be the freedom of a supernova.

Be the author of your own notes
and between them
pour your solar-panoramic audacious breath.

(First published in *Re-Membering*)

Weave Your Outrageous Image

You see, they must put things
in between you and your thread.

How else can they recruit you
to sew up their dream?

Without the mounds of dirt
thrown over your warp and woof

how could you become the face of forgetfulness
and follow someone else's thread?

Jog your memory:
There can be NOTHING
in between
that you do not allow.

Your one holy precept:
Do not abandon thy luminous thread.

Get clear of the dirt
and take the thread in your hand.

They will see your wondrous thing
and will understand

or not.

They may cast twisted eyes
laughing
or empty blinking silence
upon your vast design
or even banish you—

but only from the houses
to which you don't belong.

It matters not.

Because some—by seeing
your intricate threading—
will begin to forget
their own forgetting

and you, my friend, can continue weaving
your outrageous image into the world.

(First published in *Re-Membering*)

Flashes Buried Here

There are flashes buried here
in the hot sand of this life

Some are mirages
others are mirrors

some are red-hot miracles
awaiting the eye of your heart.

Who put them there
is not for us to know

it's not a place to dwell, but sometimes
you must cross the dry desert
to find your freedom sunrise

Even though it's been shining
through that ache within an ache
the whole time

If the rare hare has it
and the sagebrush is lush
and the moon shower
brings the cactus flower

you have absolutely no right to just lie down
and bury your head in the sand

Keep gathering the impossible shimmerings—
Some are mirages
some are mirrors
and some are red-hot miracles
awaiting the eye of your heart...

39

A Crack and Hidden Yes

Even the fabulously defeated
Coiled and feeling beaten
Wintered in and pinned with pain
Can't help but open up again

Have a crack and hidden yes
All's not black amidst the mess
Has a soft under the hard
And a heal for every scar

Protect the core...for sure, for sure
Bending inward so as not to bleed
But done with Love is done with life
And Light needs dark as dark needs Light

Its inner arms reaching out
Past the wound, past the doubt
And finds a way to come and play
The voice within as if to say:

We have a crack and hidden yes
All's not black amidst the mess
We will not coil hard and tight
We'll find the touch, and let the light

Inside the Biggest Wave

If I ever had a daughter
her name would be Undula
from 'unda' in Latin meaning wave,
to move with a smooth wavelike motion
to rise and fall,
    surge and swell,
        heave and ripple,
    billow flow and roll,
wind and wobble,
        oscillate,
    fluctuate.

Of a leaf, to have a wavy surface or edge.
'Undula' is a wavelet
and when you pronounce her d softly like a j,
it gives a Hindi sound
like Angela.

Anja is a female name meaning grace
and also in Russian and Hungarian
though in the latter two it is pronounced Anya
softer yet
instead of with the j
and means mother.

I'd name her Anya, if I ever had a daughter.

Tell me about giving birth.
Was it a surge, a swell, a heave?
And afterwards, did you sleep?

If I ever had a daughter
her name would be Anja

In the Berber language Anja means rhythm
or melody
related in sound to 'onja'
meaning to taste, test, investigate
in Swahili

and if I ever had a daughter
I would name her Onja

But I do have many daughters
little undulitas
and my little Anjitas grow up so fast

Their parents are the big ocean
and parts of me
I don't dare make small
by naming

We are constantly consummating
and therefore always pregnant.

But you can't always be pregnant, right?
That can't be good for a body.

The Ocean has a deeper womb.
The Cosmos even deeper.
Inside the Biggest Wave — the Unlimited Unda
there's a secret ecstasy

So of course it's going to hurt
when the contractions come

But those big wet undulations
on those first days of summer
when light is Queen
and the giant waves of energy rush

from within like a geyser
pouring through bodily like some deep howl
of anguish and joy—
it can't be contained

Cue the grunting and face contortions
that shape of giving birth
and the screams arrive out loud
for a change

and I worry the neighbors will hear
me giving birth
to my little undulitas.

Dear Sacred Fool

Pitter patter puzzled prayer
everywhen and everywhere

Downside up and upside down
Dreaming like a trickster clown

With mystery and bit of luck
Your sacred fool will run amuck

Oh my my and oh hell yes
Baby put on your best excess

Oh my mind and oh my my
Your wilted words will have to die

This lovely language can be cruel
Caging all our sacred fools

So be rabid rambled trip and tremble
Strike in awe at all the symbols

Inside out and outside in
freaky faerie ways to win

Full moon comes and shakes you loose
Hunt your shadow, kill your Zeus

So sin and spin and sin again
Past the gates that lock you in

Make machete magic moments
Pressing playful primal pawprints

Then pitter patter poet hammer
Let your sacred fool a'yammer

Like a purple pirate peasant
Playing in the perfect present

Receiving the True Arrows

One might think the objective is to pierce the bullseye.

Cluster the hits and win the prize.

But what if we are in fact the target?

Being hunted by a purpose we've been in the habit of hiding from?

What if there is a grander and more beautiful conspiracy between the arrow and the bow arm, the feathers and the wind, the target and the heart, to conjoin disparate and wild elements, conjuring new quests and questions?

What if all along we've been winning at the wrong tournaments?

What if, before the string is even released, we stretch our everything, refine our silences, open all our ears, and cultivate our heart as sacred space for receiving the true arrows?

A MIND OF THEIR OWN

"You can't use up creativity.
The more you use the more you have."
—Maya Angelou

No Time For Poetry

For putting bare feet on the ground
(No) Time

For hearing the morning's sound
(No) Time

For having night over for tea
(No) Time

For not to do but to be
(No) Time

For friends for fun for free
(No) Time

For what the spider spun
(No)Time

For what the moon has sung
(No) Time

For runes called clouds and tunes called trees
(No)Time

For taking questions for a walk
(No) Time

For listening to the river talk
(No) Time

Poems Are Lurking Everywhere

Is it that poems hide from us or that we hide from
poems? The truth is, poems are lurking everywhere.

I just stepped on one this morning,
wasn't looking where I was going.

Ran into a redwood—the last remaining old growth.

Or was it that I was ONLY looking where I was going?

That's a good way to miss where you need to go.

One jumped out at me on the bus
from the eviction signs
at Here There
on the border between everything
singing, "just let me live!"

I tipped my coffee cup
and found one clinging to the rim,
asking for a drink.

So addicted, these poems are
to being heard

that they'll even drop in
on your conversation with a friend
and interject their opinion,
whether you want it or not

and shout at you for a 3 AM feeding.

"What's so important that it can't wait
until morning, like a reasonable person?"

I ask, like an unreasonable person.

It responds, "I'll tell you, how much time you got?"

"Ok, OK! I'm all ears,"

It starts reciting before I can even get in a yawn.

Turns out it's just something about
life and death
love and fear
rabbits and nostalgia
moons and grandfathers
prisons and power
bows and arrows
pain and plastic shit-bags
teachers and wind
dancing and watersheds
eagles and reciprocity,

Nothing much.

I go back to sleep,
but I can feel the lumps of poems
lurking in my pillow.

They'll just have to wait until morning, I think.

But when dawn arrives, they're no longer here.

Oh well, all the poems hiding in the sky
and mud and streets await.

Train Surfer

This poem will resist metaphor,
hyperbole will be an absolute last recourse
and extraneous details will be discarded.

It will convey only what is right in front of me
and not only that, but what is the essence of it.

Which in this case is a woman standing on the train
(to where is bland)
coffee mug in her hand
(which one is irrelevant here)
taking a wide stance to avoid falling (literally)
with the shifting sway of the car
from a seemingly drunken conductor.

We've been on here for nearly four years
and I find myself liking the way she surfs the train
in her black Adidas and braids
nonchalant and professional
with no book, no music, no phone
to distract her from the moment.

Like this commute is the killer wave.

She doesn't even resort to writing a silly poem
about the man in a red shirt
watching her surf.

Extravagant Hooves

{From late Middle English (in the sense 'unusual, unsuitable'): from medieval Latin extravagant- 'diverging greatly', from the verb extravagari, from Latin extra- 'outside' + vagari 'wander'.}.

With extravagant hooves you walk outside
even the perimeter

pounding pavement until you find the free dirt

the world's a hot and heavy
aching anchor today

With sobbing soul and throbbing soles
you just want to feel
something raw, something real

with grit and gawd
beyond the mind, beyond the grind

So you hang a thumb out to the world

until a free syllable catches a ride
on a wild-eyed word
hitching with barely a hitch

A few go by, but one slows and rolls
down its tinted windows
and with a voice so suave, says

"Jump in the back of my 4x4 metaphor,
I'll take you up the hill."

So you hop on, feeling the wind flow
through your long curly verse

Soon you're free of the city
where gravity and noise sit on thrones

like bloodthirsty despots
colonizing every last paragraph of the world

laying its stink upon you
like a colossal cologne.

There is no gravity up in the wind.

Up where language matters.
Or doesn't.

Up where a phrase on the breeze
is more meaningful than whole libraries
in the valley haze.

Up here you're an aerated acrobat—
even with such extravagant hooves
you can dance like bee.

Forest Poet

They're casting for the role of forest poet

I wanna play the part
and live among the redwood trees
weaving words like vines
that look into the face of love and fear

it's only slightly mad

not on any high school
career-planning curriculum
or drop-down menu

I wanna play the part of the forest poet
and have morning tea with animal allies
and titillating conversations with flowing creeks

wanna compose poems as medicine
for a world caught up

a bit strange they say

stranger than sports fans rioting
black Friday madness
or making gas-powered leaf-blowers
landmines
or little plastic scented trees for cars?

stranger than hating others
because of where they are from
or what they look like
or who they love?

so let others play the part of
politician,
programmer,
engineer,
janitor,
office manager
military officer,
designer,
carpenter,
athlete,
mailman,
gadget-maker.

They've all got their place.

It's just that I wanna play the part of the forest poet

Is it needed any less?

The Ones You Threw Away

I want to know the ones you threw away
that couldn't find their true form

in order to come to term
to take their first breath screaming

what was the ardent word seed
that impregnated the first syllabic

egg that no eyes have ever seen?
that's what I want to know

A Sea-Scented Poem Jumped Off the Edge of the West

Standing up on the west end
tongue tasting the salty wind

I try to shake the shore from my everywhere

it's going to be impossible to get all the grains
out from under the fingernails of these palabras

the playa played me
painting me the pigment of three shades of shale

I wonder, which part of this sea-scented poem
wants to be part of a larger conversation:

these sand-speckled sentences
or the ocean-blown space
between all the words

that

just

jump

off

the

cliff....?

This Poem Must Be Upgraded

Consumer desires must be met

So this poem must be upgraded:
a nipple falls out of its dress
it contradicts the status quo
it bares its whiteness on a skeleton

It promises you youth and vigor
a happy wife with morning dew,
a larger cock that never fails

An easier life, security and red roses everyday
thorns not included

They must be fed, these engines slick with future
forever on their radar

These stomachs with black hole hands

But alas, the stomachs do not find eternal sunshine
and believe they've failed

No jobs have been created from this poem
No economy boosted

No youth restored, no wisdom gained,
other than whatever is wrestled from it
with whys and wonder

A Mind of Its Own

I attempt an observation,
precise and aloof,

but it runs away to Uruguay
all moody and judgmental

I try to put a hat and tie on it, daring debonair—
it runs around in its underwear

It starts as a walk in the vacant street
then pulls all the world aside
to do cartwheels with the kids

A simple ode is simple enough
one would think

until it props itself up
on a pile of grievances

Or inserts its cheery balm
when a lament is what was ordered

One tear gets you ten,
so serious that something
puts its foot out to trip me
raucous laughter from the bushes

it makes one suspect that a poem
has a mind of its own

How Poems Arrive

They arrive like coyotes calling at 2am
during the Full Cold Moon

I step outside to gather
the yellow and orange leaves
that the fierce winter wind has thrown
to the ground with such a fury
that I miss most of them

but some I catch
and arrange in a pattern
not as pretty as they looked on the tree
but I'd rather them not go to waste

poems can arrive like those
little waves on the lake
after the duck lands

or a barely audible whisper
from an ancient grove

or louder, like a chorus of crickets
the rush of a river, a flow over eager falls

A poem can burst open like a seed

or often just settle in slowly
like a deep breath
climbing up spirally
like a bean vine around the pole of you

Bright and Awe-full Symphony of Things

From an ancient spruce these forms float up

like a black flock
writing sleet-soaked secrets
into the silvery winter sky

Faster than sound, they chirp
a slickening thunder
woven with a frightening light

so close even your cloven bones
run up a lucky tree seeking shelter
called love, fearful

of getting struck.

But it's no use—
The tree conspires with the throat of birds
whose wild words
are wrapped in a destiny
in which there is no safety zone.

So you might as well let loose
your copper raptor
into the moonless night unknown
and soar beside them

You might as well stretch
your thirsty ears on their lambent wings

lending your glistening feathers
to the bright and awe-full symphony of things.

OF MOSQUITOES, MAKERS, AND THE MACHINE

"To be a poet is a condition, not a profession."
—Robert Frost

Widening As You Dip
(for Hart Crane)

Yes, Ralph, you asked
for a national poet made to order

And Walt, you were at his door
before the ink dried,

singing a new song—
a song of yourself and all of us

Hart, you followed in lilac footsteps
as bard of American affirmation

but you couldn't abide an utter Wasteland
so you launched your circular canticles

against all the Eliotic ennui
casting a wide net and even wider bridge

spanning both the past and the future
supporting both the grass and the machine

the bold task of a would-be redeemer
but it could not bear the weight of darkness

laughing twice as hard,
drinking twice as much

despite some song of your soul declaring:
Imagination is beyond despair

you threw yourself on the bent foam and wave
a voyage that would never find its end

sailing out of port into cold waters
you broke your tower on azure seas

yet widening us even as you dip
your spindrift gaze spins us toward paradise

Mary Oliver's Truancy

Only record she ever broke
was for skipping school
because the Ohio hills
had more to teach her
than her teachers

Or her broken home
red rage running
from her dark family of things
to which she didn't belong

Wandering the forest with Whitman
in her knapsack
hunting fish and clams
berries and words

She traveled to the moon and back
with a pencil—
her one wild and precious life

Giving the world 50,000 words
foraged from the landscape
lining the pockets of hungry souls

We now have a thousand mornings
of wild geese
and big-eyed grasshoppers
calling our soft animal bodies home
loving on bright summer days
because of Mary Oliver's truancy.

Lament for the Makers

A tribute to several artists: Bill Withers, John Prine, Ursula Le Guin, Leonard Cohen, Toni Morrison, Mary Oliver. Modeled after Scottish poet Dunbar's Lament for the Makers, each stanza ends with, "Timor mortis conturbat me," or "The fear of death disturbs me." What would we do without the makers?

The strong unmerciful tyrant takes
All that will and desire makes
Down to that great and dark deep sea.
Timor mortis conturbat me.

What's built up must come down
The ruin of all laurel crowns
The fall of all pageantry.
Timor mortis conturbat me.

All the songs sung in the day
Will in the night be swept away
And embrace the fateful darkening.
Timor mortis conturbat me.

She says Love is or Love ain't
Love's not cute nor constrained
Thin love ain't no love at all
Night befalls and death will call
So make your love robust and free.
Timor mortis conturbat me.

Ain't no sunshine when he's gone
Who'll be your friend to carry on?
Just call on me brother, lean on me.
Timor mortis conturbat me.

Give us one thing we can hold on to
Perhaps a dream, a song or two
Make us an angel that flies from Montgomery.
Timor mortis conturbat me.

Beautiful Loser sang Hallelujah
He sang it dark, but not to fool ya
He rang the bells that could be rung
And sung with dark but golden tongue
But then the end as meant to be.
Timor mortis conturbat me.

Every third thought shall be the grave
And all that we attempt to save
Will be sunk in the unknowable sea.
Timor mortis conturbat me.

All the art and artifice wrought
Falls to the ground to finally rot
Then fades into the Final Dream.
Timor mortis conturbat me.

There's more we want to hear and see
More we want to make believe
Much more we want to love and be.
Timor mortis conturbat me.

But the end is built into it all
The makers' splendid fires fall
To ashes and the embers cool
With death as the final school
A hard and ruthless finality.
Timor mortis conturbat me.

Strange Birds
(for Robinson Jeffers)

Such strange birds
perched on the shoreline
these heavy poets chirping lightly
for whom squares will not do.

They are in it for the curves only.

The shoreline keeps shape-shifting—
that is the key to the rest.

The shoreline is a sentinel against forgetting
and if you don't understand the shoreline

how can you understand the human heart?
they say.

So they perch on the Pacific
and purchase peaceful poems
with their spoondrift ears

Sometimes they fall on their head
listening to the vast subterranean love-beats
building things:

For the hawk within, stone towers
for the multitudes within, stone benches
for the child within, feather ships

Between dinner and dessert
a drop from the great voyage
drips on a napkin

And still we clean our chins with it
Scribbling scribbling

on the black island in the storm
in the crowd, on the sea
in the trenches of a world asunder
in the mines
from the glowburn night
on the backs of whales

the music wafts in from every direction
and the notes are untranslatable

Yet we hunger for syllables of understanding

How curious that petal-soft verse
is sometimes harder than granite...
and holds us up
like a fat bird on the ocean gale

Chirp chirp for us you strange birds
with sounds carved from rocks and flesh
and all the slight angles of our ancient dispositions

Chirp your inimitable chirp
you strange birds

Chirp chirp and make our flesh
cha cha with goosebumps

(First published in *Re-Membering*)

On Mosquitoes and Poets

I love all creatures. Is something people say but don't
mean it. Like, off with mosquitoes. And the tiny
bloodsucking equine they rode in on. Yet still, here's my
ode to them, an anthological poetic potpourri and
bestiary:

Ever the gentleman Berry
(Wendell, of Kentucky)—
knowing a thing or two about sacred things
and forgiveness—bowed and said,

"I beg your pardon, come here
and I will kill thee,
holy though thou art."

That Surface Dweller, Saint of the Dirt,
then murdered the Needle-Nosed Bastard.

Ms. Oliver (may she rest in poetry),
ever the gentlewoman,
dedicated a poem to the wasp
that stung her

Neruda with his ode to bees had sung:
"Oh, the multitudes!"

In the Rock-n-Roll years
the remaining Doors sang a mariachi song

"No me moleste mosquito,
just let me eat my burrito,
why don't you just go home?"

summing up the sentiment
in most people's hearts
true feelings about the proboscised ones

though it really was just an excuse
to jam for a few minutes
without the Lizard King.

Dolphins and dogs
all get their due

elephants and bats,
even a spider or two

but lonely mosquito, what can you do?—
no one talks about you

all nightingales and pretty birds
must be quite puffed up by now
with obsequious herds
offering vain verses and bows

and so I thought I'd gather them up,
these pesky people, with faces
not even a mother could love

alongside the green valley loons
lavender dawns and summer moons
all roses-are-reds, and all that's blue,
and sing their praises, (or if none be found)
then at least their due.

But that poor cup o' tea priest Issa
beat me to it
with his rascal haiku feasts:

driven
from
next
door
come
on
in
mosquitos

only fleas and flies
compete more for Issa's eyes

But for my money, mosquito
owes a verse of gratitude first
to First Person Sorrowful Ko Un
—ever the epic democrat (lower case d)

while in prison he made an oath
that every person he had ever met
would be remembered in a poem:

"I've been bitten by a mosquito
thanks a million.
Why, I'm really alive,
scratch, scratch."

nailed it
(the subject, not the insect)

Redemption therein lies
for the mosquitos' lives

Some facts you can't improve upon.

The Poet's Assent

The poet Rainer Maria Rilke has been some sort of koan for me. February is the time of year that was a creative hurricane for Rilke, allowing him to finish the Sonnets to Orpheus and the Duino Elegies in 1922. In one week, Rilke completed the unfinished elegies, and from February 2 to February 23, Rilke completed all the 55 sonnets of the two parts of Sonnets to Orpheus

He then wrote to his long-time friend, the inimitable Lou Andreas-Salomé, that he had finished "everything in a few days; it was a boundless storm, a hurricane of the spirit, and whatever inside me is like thread and webbing, framework, it all cracked and bent. No thought of food."

Once I threw myself into understand the heart of Rilke, his poetic motive and mission, as it were. This is a poetic attempt to get at some of what I think he was up to and how he got there. In the meantime, I am still diving in.

"Incline a while," she said with a smile.
A simple life, simply styled,

so with legs outstretched and peering into
the Poet's mind and querying:

what's this queer soul really hearing?
what's this mirror really mirroring?

Seeing into things and Being
into emptiness beauty fleeing

The whole of his heart's work
from the hole in his heart works

because he dug and dug for days
and found upon his tongue a praise

Upon a summer solstice morn
on the eve of the World War
a poet bent his inner ear
and found the point drawing near

Descended deep until he found
a limit to his seeing eye
no more secrets could be spied
until he looked with loving eyes

without it there would not be
the Sonnets or the Elegies

Only with that descending tone
could he ascend - not merely up
but with the whole earth on its throne
and with an ear so different bent
with drums began: "ASSENT! ASSENT!"

Only heart bent circling love
could form a praise upon a tongue
could a faithful Yes be a sung
like a song from mourning dove

Only then the jailbreak
of those images locked within
and from behind the bars of time
the Poet affirms the world again

See-Feel

Some writers/artists practice acute observations about how they create, where inspiration emerges, and can, in addition, articulate that.

I haven't possessed that skill, not having turned my attention precisely on the 'how'. I'm trying to look more closely, to illuminate some of the organic how of it.

So: If I get real quiet, right now in this moment, I can "hear" any number of species/elements: roots, cloud, moss forest, dew drop, beetle, red rock, fern spore, star fish, waves crashing, frog, black fog of fear within white supremacy, scent of pennyroyal, log burning, your sacred shining wound, fir needle...

And that's just this moment. It can be as minute as the lungs of a leaf or as 'abstract' as the Earth as giant metabolizing sacred slug beast.

Then sometimes, I "tune into" and deepen the "hearing" of a particular experience, and it unfurls from there.

But by 'hear' I don't mean I hear talking, certainly not in words, as in eavesdropping on a conversation.

Even when transliterated into English, for example, "sea speaks its longing to moon, as ever-turning tide," the 'speaking' is almost always a placeholder for a robust interiority and lived experience, interdependence with the lived experiences of others.

Permeability becomes possibility.

It is also not mere translation of a visual observation or even other sense experience, though that can coalesce part of a final form.

My experience is that I "see-feel" as in I'm inside bodies. But it's not really 'I' over here and experience some 'thing' over there—I AM that embodiment. I 'see-feel' urges and interiority from within. The felt-sense is almost always accompanied by what I can only describe as a longing, an eros, a movement, a striving, as it relates, plays, wrestles, eats, is eaten by, its 'environment'.

All this then gets transliterated mytho-poetically into words.

Alas, I am very poor translator, so if anything arrives that approaches being 'decent' poem or writing, it is because the subjectivity I 'see-feel' seems to want to take on the form as an alternate identity. Almost as if it is shapeshifting or time-traveling, to be known in different ways.

And everything and everywho wants to be known.

The extent to which the result is flat, is the extent to which 'I' have got in the way of the 'hearing.'

So that's some end of the year morning dew.

Pregnancy and Poetry

"With light and dark your destined orbit's marked—
Wax gibbous and grow a pregnant shaping
Of some image towards unfurled freedom"
—Madam Eclipse

Mama bears give birth in the middle of winter, in the den of hibernation. Though they are inseminated in the summer, they can delay implanting what will become the growing fetus until they are fat enough before hibernation. That is, they can choose the shape of their pregnancy. Or she can abort, reabsorbing her fertilized egg. A lot depends on what support she has. If she has sufficient lipid layers and a cozy den, and other factors probably only known to her, she'll continue to wax gibbous, and in January or February she'll unfurl furry little babies the size of squirrels.

In a dead of December dream, a friend called Felix/Felicia is very pregnant, and we're in a room talking with their wife about possible birthing scenarios— doulas, hospital, home-birth. But the wife likewise sees them as a friend, not seeming to recognize them, despite their bright eyes. We're looking at an old picture of them when they were newlyweds, when she was pregnant, and my friend played the role of a he/him and doting husband and father-to-be.

Nostalgia for innocence mixed with heaping tablespoons of wondrous possibility fill the room.

I awake to scattered scurries of rain and a delicious darkness.

In this stretched pregnant hour before the dance of the day, this hushed unrushed, this unseen hanging chill clings a damp cloak skin tight on the fog face hymn of dawn, while stars still sing soliloquies.

The Silence is practically swimmable.

I stretch my back into it and float.

I pour pitch black down my poor back
and feel my arch grow towards some image
of unfurled freedom.

Apprentice to the Archer's Art

I pull back the string of me
and take aim:

Honing my energy into a field-point
I practice shooting the arrows of me

The target is my heart
The target is your heart

The target is the sacred wound
where the true treasure's found

I'm hunting wholeness and wild purpose
I'm stalking shining shadows and deep belongings

The wind made a quiver of me
full of fletchéd arrows

The wisdom of my wayward feet
bent a bow from all my errors

My apprenticeship continues—
patient practice plays its part, but

the heart of the archer's art
is love and wild Eros

Poetry and the Machine

There's a line from Hart Crane from nearly 100 years ago that haunts me; not from his poetry but from his thoughts about what poetry could, should do:

"Unless poetry can absorb the machine then it has failed."

This lays down a gauntlet, a rather daunting one. Crane, like us, was living at a time of accelerated socio-technological change—Wall Street, skyscrapers and other architectural marvels, personal vehicles, blessings and diseases of affluenza, world war. All of which were absorbed in his stunning attempt, 'The Bridge'.

What is meant by absorb? To absorb is different than address or critique. It's even something different than Ferlinghetti's "Poetry destroys the bad breath of machines," one of many hyperbolic purposes attributed to this thing called poetry.

Still…

What *is* poetry's niche in the ecosystem of cultural shapeshifting?

At minimum, poetry must grapple with the forces of its age, then perhaps turn them to aesthetic, if not liberatory ends. An earthier way of putting it: art rooted equally in the times and in vision.

Taking Crane's criteria seriously now, it would mean absorbing among other recent manifestations of The Machine: Robot dogs used by US Border control;

billionaire wannabe sky-kings and an $11 million gold cube installed as 'art' in NYC as a gimmick to sell NFTs (read: stunts of late-stage capitalism); the murder of black people in no-knock warrants; insta-everything hijacking our attention and our wallets; the reality of these tech platforms connecting so many people but also selling your eyeballs; AI infiltrating nearly every platform, profession; and the ongoing genocides, ecocides, and the specter of the imperial boomerang— that is, the core and peripheral violence that subsidizes it all.

But to bring this to a personal meaning: it must absorb my experience of that flashpoint where Empire meets Anti-Empire, whether in streets of Chicago or Oakland confronting a political ruling elite's shiny sales pitch of the new and improved, same ol' same ol' status quo and its enforcement arm, or the watersheds of up north Minnesota, where State-Capital-Police converge as a 3-Headed hound and one finally understands The Machine and its function (consume everything in its path, including those who are driving it), where that energy of "take, control, destroy" meets the energy of the voice of water and a million ancestral prayers, of birdsong and memories of home, and the unconquerable coalescence of heartbreak and love.

Absorb THAT. Digest THAT. Metabolize THAT. Transmute THAT.

This is what poetry might do. I won't say it's failed until it does so, only that this is one niche that it can fulfill. And I can't help but feel, a vitally important one.

So I agree with Crane, knowing too well that to let it in may destroy you because that is the only thing The

Machine knows. The only way to digest The Machine without being destroyed is to fulfill that other function deemed necessary by all manner of poets and mystics and prophets from Keats to King, 'an extraordinary capacity for surrender.'

Crane meant surrender to all sensations and the accidents of language.

For me in this era, it invites a surrender to and rootedness in the full spectrum of reality-based (earth-rooted) mythopoetic ecospiritual entanglement, without which, we are likely the ones to be digested.

Accepting this is offering a yearning Yes to the metabolizing meta-machine called poetry.

These Words Have Accomplished Nothing

They say that poetry is the language closest to the
mystic's path. The paradox remains: the urge to express
in words what simply cannot be expressed.

The nature of a word is to reveal what may be hidden,
but in its revealing it simultaneously obscures. By
necessity it leaves things out. By necessity it shapes
what is to be seen, and by doing so, creates the illusion
of having presented reality.

For us two-legged scribblers, no matter how perfectly
plucked from the autumn air, words seem bricks
beyond which hides that which will not submit to form.

Is not a blank page more honest?

Silence more true?

Shall I take all these words back? Have they
accomplished anything at all?

Yet, is it any different than awkward golden warbler—
that friendly feathered mystic—
who doesn't *know* how to express Source in Birdness,
but does anyway?

Or cherry blossom mystic,
flirting with how to say ONE LOVE
in February with fluent Flowerness?

She does her level best,
but the constraints of the season
are a givenness that pins her in.

Each petal a word of her clumsy, gorgeous poem.

All cute and pathetic, like you and me.

But Oh, the results!

ABOUT THE AUTHOR

Ryan Van Lenning, M.A., is author of *Trust the Ceremony, F*ck the Ceremony, Trust the Ceremony, One Bright and Real Caress, From Inside These Wild*

Ones, An Ambitious Silence, Within the Cave Something Pulses, Re-Membering: Poems of Earth and Soul, and a collection of haiku, *High-Cooing Through the Seasons*. His new collections *Becoming Beautiful Barbarians* and *Riverever* will be released throughout 2025-26. He is the 2019 recipient of Jodi Stutz Poetry Award by Toyon Literary Magazine and his poetry appears in various poetry journals and the book *A Walk with Nature: Poetic Encounters That Nourish the Soul* and *Behind the Mask: 40 Quarantine Poems from Humboldt County*.

Ryan is Founder of Wild Nature Heart, supporting people to re-connect with the wisdom of both inner and outer wild nature, to live their callings into the world, and to assist in the work of repairing broken belonging during this Great Turning. He is a teacher, ecotherapist and wilderness rite-of-passage guide and lives among the forests and rivers of Northern California. He facilitates 6-week workshops called Write Your Wild River, Earth Intimacies, and Deep Belonging a couple times a year.

ABOUT WILD NATURE HEART

Wild Nature Heart supports people to connect with the wisdom of inner and outer wild nature, to embody our wholeness, and to live our wild purpose into the world in order to inhabit our particular niche in the ecosystem of healing and justice. Through 1-on-1 ecotherapy, earth-rooted mentoring, custom and group wilderness rite-of-passage ceremonies, and various Deep Belonging courses, workshops, and seasonal gatherings, Wild Nature Heart cultivates an ecospirituality that nourishes our deep belonging in the animate web of life in order to do the decolonial work that we are called to do in this moment of the Great Turning.

Wild Nature Heart believes that to cross this threshold into species maturity with a next-season guest pass we must keep our imaginations robust and make moves that subvert inherited paradigms of fear and supremacy. We are being invited to fall through the inherited maps into new territories towards collective liberation. As crises continue to invite us across thresholds of initiation, we crack open the paved highways of our hearts and bodies to allow the tributaries of our holy longings and wild purpose to flow in and out.

The journey is both a daily and life-long practice, as much as it is multi-generational and multi-species. We practice simultaneously being both death doulas to the world that is dying and birth doulas to the one being born. _www.wildnatureheart.com_

TITLES IN THE *RE-MEMBERING* SERIES

The book that began it all:
Re-Membering: Poems of Earth and Soul

The 75 poems in *Re-Membering* are an unabashed celebration of the sensuality of wild nature. Redwoods reach without apology towards the sky, and rivers flow with unflagging energy towards the ocean. This collection re-members Ryan's personal explorations into wild nature, but it also re-collects for all of us a time when our kinship and inter-connectedness with the natural world was self-evident, and invites us to fully re-inhabit and say "Yes!" to our sensual natures, our animal bodies, our playfulness and creativity, connection, mystery, and our instinctive love for this beautiful, sentient Earth.

"Ryan's poetry speaks deeply and clearly to the awakening to our true interconnected nature, which is the only way we can transform our world."
—Molly Young Brown, author of *Coming Back to Life: The Updated Guide to the Work That Reconnects* (co-authored with Joanna Macy)

One Bright and Real Caress
Book 2 in the *Re-Membering* Series

Build an altar at each moment with a goodbye on the tip of the tongue. Slow dance drunk in the robust now. Show up with playful paws the gravity of worms. Strap the searchlight around your ribs and shuffle like a crescent moon over all your little resistances. Can we be here now? Really be here?

These are some of the invitations lurking in the poems of *One Bright and Real Caress*. This collection is a celebration of the moment. Of not escaping. Of impermanence. Of death as life partner. With syllables of relentless affirmation, these poems bring an unconditional caress over all the textures of life and our multitudes within. As an invitation to presence and an honoring of the all-too-real struggle to not flee the moment, *One Bright and Real Caress* welcomes every conceivable crescent mood, slivered and slow, with no aim but to edge out more and more into the whole ceremony and celebration.

From Inside These Wild Ones
Book 3 in the *Re-Membering* Series

Gorgeous Storm

This gorgeous storm
keeps getting stuck in my teeth

as if I could bite-size my way
to destiny

When all I want
is to have it come
racing out my lungs

Like a waterfall plunging
over my luscious tongue

flooding all the landscapes
of my crooked life.

to join the wrens and warblers
and beloved lusts
of a wounded world
washing away the old debris

Please, Storm, please,
knock down the weak branches
of my being

Prune me for the season
I am meant to live

EXCERPTS FROM THE AUTHOR'S OTHER BOOKS

An Ambitious Silence

What it calls for is an elegant unraveling—
more accurate
and stunning than ever before

sinking into an ambitious silence,
robust and cunning

Do something useful for a change—Listen
so deep and richly
the big ear wants to open through you, remembering
all.

Be unfashionable—tear the ears off the false notes.

Shake your feathers and invite the fox and raven

Until oak reaches into you
and the deep waters gather.

Mud and Moon are your Elders.
You won't get far without them.

Chant Old Man Owl and Sister Dawn unto you.
That ancient place within beckons.

Unfold it into your bones
and drum your skeletal fragments
until they dance.

Then, like a humble apprentice
pay the tuition for your truth

bartering for the next bold season
with the currency of your heart

letting an unreasonable love
claim you like a throne

and walk your blessed seduction home.

From *Trust the Ceremony, F*ck the Ceremony, Trust the Ceremony*

Door-To-Mystery-Knows-Where

There is a door to Mystery-knows-where
and you are being invited to step through

The new doorway through which you pass
is framed with grander questions

where you'll pick up pieces left
in your canyons long ago

and find on the side
fragments resting by the fire

drinking ale for an evening tale
of dreams wanting to find their flesh

Put them in your wide-brim hat
and home in on your succulent belonging

becoming an obsessionate one
like a convict who loves their fate

This is the door to Mystery-knows-where
and you are being invited through

From *Becoming Beautiful Barbarians*
(Forthcoming)

Off-Script

This is not a dress rehearsal.

This is an undress rehearsal—
We're undressing the stories
we've rehearsed for far too long.

This is not a blockbuster movie.

This is composter cinema—
The only heroes that will be rushing in
are the ones we see naked
in the morning mirror.

And that is more than enough.

With thistles and a raven's beak
we tear up the scripts we inherited.

They are what got us into the Big Trouble.

Liberation is leaking out
of every page of the book we are writing.

There is no script worth a damn
that doesn't include the voice of the river
the cries of our ancestors
or the longings living in our bones.

For each mouthful of empty-calorie modernity,
we create a meal
of new melodies.

For each megabyte of consumption,
we create a terabyte
of participatory dreaming.

With each breath we forge
strange and novel toys
in service to the Grand Metabolism.
We are preparing a buffet of the future.